Table of Contents

The Original All-Bran® Muffins

PREP TIME: 20 minutes ■ **TOTAL TIME: 50 minutes**

Makes 12 muffins

1¼	cups all-purpose flour
½	cup sugar
1	tablespoon baking powder
¼	teaspoon salt
2	cups *Kellogg's® All-Bran®* Original Cereal
1¼	cups non-fat milk
1	egg
¼	cup vegetable oil

1. Stir together flour, sugar, baking powder and salt. Set aside.

2. In large mixing bowl, combine KELLOGG'S ALL-BRAN cereal and milk. Let stand about 2 minutes or until cereal softens. Add egg and oil. Beat well. Add flour mixture, stirring only until combined. Portion evenly into twelve 2½-inch muffin-pan cups coated with cooking spray.

3. Bake at 400°F about 20 minutes or until golden brown. Serve warm.

VARIATIONS:
• For muffins with reduced calories, fat and cholesterol, use 2 tablespoons sugar, 2 tablespoons oil and substitute 2 egg whites for 1 egg.
• For muffins with reduced fat and cholesterol, substitute 2 egg whites for 1 egg and ¼ cup sweetened applesauce (or 2-ounce jar bananas baby food) for ¼ cup vegetable oil. (Muffin texture may vary slightly from the Original ALL-BRAN Muffins recipe.)

Peanut Butter Fudge Brownies

PREP TIME: 15 minutes ■ **TOTAL TIME: 40 minutes**

Makes 16 servings

- ¾ cup all-purpose flour
- 1 cup sugar
- ½ teaspoon baking powder
- 2 squares (1 ounce each) unsweetened baking chocolate
- ⅓ cup margarine or butter
- 1 cup *Kellogg's Raisin Bran*® Cereal
- ¼ cup creamy peanut butter
- ¼ cup milk
- 2 eggs
- 1 teaspoon vanilla extract

1. Stir together flour, sugar and baking powder. Set aside.

2. In 2-quart saucepan, melt chocolate and margarine over very low heat, stirring constantly. Remove from heat. Cool slightly. Add KELLOGG'S RAISIN BRAN cereal, peanut butter, milk, eggs and vanilla. Mix well. Stir in flour mixture. Spread evenly in 8×8×2-inch baking pan coated with cooking spray.

3. Bake at 325°F about 30 minutes or until tests done. Cool completely before serving.

Lemony Apple Salad

PREP TIME: 10 minutes   ■   **TOTAL TIME: 10 minutes**

Makes 6 servings

½ cup lemon low-fat yogurt

1 tablespoon finely snipped fresh parsley

2 cups cubed, unpeeled red apples (2 medium)

½ cup thinly sliced celery

½ cup seedless red grapes, halved

½ cup *Kellogg's® All-Bran®* Original Cereal or ½ cup
Kellogg's® All-Bran® Bran Buds® Cereal

6 lettuce leaves

1. In medium bowl, combine yogurt and parsley. Stir in apples, celery and grapes. Cover and refrigerate until ready to serve.

2. Just before serving, stir in KELLOGG'S ALL-BRAN cereal. Serve on lettuce leaves.

Cinnamon Easy's

PREP TIME: 20 minutes ■ **TOTAL TIME: 1 hour 45 minutes**

Makes 12 servings

 3 **tablespoons margarine, melted**
 ⅔ **cup firmly packed brown sugar**
 ½ **cup dark corn syrup**
 ½ **cup pecan halves**
 1 **teaspoon ground cinnamon**
 ¼ **cup firmly packed brown sugar**
 2 **packages (¼ ounce each) active dry yeast**
 1¼ **cups warm water (110° to 115°F)**
 1½ **cups *Kellogg's Raisin Bran*® Cereal**
 6 **tablespoons margarine, softened and divided**
 1 **teaspoon salt**
 1 **package (3 ounces) eggs custard mix**
 3 **to 3½ cups all-purpose flour**

1. Combine first 4 ingredients in greased 13×9×2-inch baking pan. Spread evenly. Set aside. Stir together cinnamon and ¼ cup brown sugar. Set aside.

2. Dissolve yeast in warm water in large mixing bowl. Add KELLOGG'S RAISIN BRAN cereal. Let stand about 2 minutes or until cereal is softened. Add 4 tablespoons of the softened margarine, salt, and custard mix, stirring until mix is dissolved. Stir in enough flour to make a stiff dough.

3. On lightly floured surface, knead dough into an 18×12-inch rectangle. Spread the remaining 2 tablespoons softened margarine over dough. Sprinkle with cinnamon-sugar mixture. Starting from shorter side, roll up dough like a jelly roll. Seal edge. Cut into 1-inch slices. Place cut side down on pecan mixture in pan. Let rise in warm place until double in volume (about 1 hour).

4. Bake at 400°F about 25 minutes or until lightly browned. Remove from oven. Invert onto serving plate. Serve warm.

VARIATIONS: ½ cup KELLOGG'S® ALL-BRAN® cereal or KELLOGG'S ALL-BRAN BRAN BUDS® cereal may be substituted for the KELLOGG'S RAISIN BRAN cereal.

Apple Bran Muffins

PREP TIME: 20 minutes ■ **TOTAL TIME: 1 hour**

Makes 12 muffins

  2 **cups all-purpose flour**
  2 **teaspoons low-calorie granulated sugar substitute**
  1 **tablespoon baking powder**
  ½ **teaspoon salt**
  2 **cups *Kellogg's*® *All-Bran*® Original Cereal or *Kellogg's*® *All-Bran*® *Bran Buds*® Cereal**
  2 **cups apple juice**
  1 **egg**
  ¼ **cup vegetable oil**

1. Stir together flour, sugar substitute, baking powder and salt. Set aside.

2. In large mixing bowl, combine KELLOGG'S ALL-BRAN cereal and apple juice. Let stand about 2 minutes or until cereal softens. Add egg and oil. Beat well. Add flour mixture, stirring only until combined. Portion evenly into twelve 2½-inch muffin-pan cups coated with cooking spray.

3. Bake at 400°F about 26 minutes or until golden brown. Serve warm.

VARIATION: 2 cups milk may be substituted for apple juice.

Cereal Baked French Toast

PREP TIME: 10 minutes ■ **TOTAL TIME: 20 minutes**

Makes 6 servings

> 2 cups *Kellogg's® All-Bran® Complete®* **Wheat Flakes Cereal**
>
> 1 **egg**
>
> ½ **cup non-fat milk**
>
> ¼ **teaspoon salt**
>
> 6 **slices day-old whole wheat bread**

1. Crush cereal to make 1 cup. Place in shallow dish or pie plate.

2. In another shallow dish, beat egg with milk and salt. Dip bread quickly in egg mixture, turning once.

3. Coat on both sides of bread with crushed cereal and place in single layer on well greased foil-lined baking sheet. Bake in 450°F oven 10 to 15 minutes or until crisp and golden brown.

Honey Raisin Bran Muffins

PREP TIME: 10 minutes ■ **TOTAL TIME: 30 minutes**

Makes 12 muffins

> 1¾ cups all-purpose flour
> 1 tablespoon baking powder
> ¼ teaspoon salt
> 2 tablespoons sugar
> 2½ cups *Kellogg's Raisin Bran®* Cereal
> 1¼ cups non-fat milk
> ⅓ cup honey
> 1 egg
> ¼ cup vegetable oil

1. Stir together flour, baking powder, salt and sugar. Set aside.

2. In large mixing bowl, combine KELLOGG'S RAISIN BRAN cereal, milk and honey. Let stand 3 minutes or until cereal softens. Add egg and oil. Beat well. Add flour mixture, stirring only until combined. Portion batter evenly into twelve 2½-inch muffin-pan cups coated with cooking spray.

3. Bake at 400°F for 20 minutes or until lightly browned. Serve warm.

Baked Pork Chops with Corn Stuffing

PREP TIME: 25 minutes ■ **TOTAL TIME: 1 hour 10 minutes**

Makes 6 servings

- 1 **tablespoon chopped onion**
- ¼ **cup chopped celery**
- 2 **tablespoons shortening**
- 4 **cups soft bread crumbs**
- 1 **cup *Kellogg's® All-Bran® Original Cereal* or**
  1 cup *Kellogg's® All-Bran® Bran Buds® Cereal*
- 1 **teaspoon salt**
- ¼ **teaspoon pepper**
- ¼ **teaspoon poultry seasoning**
- 1 **cup canned whole kernel corn, drained**
- 1 **cup liquid drained from corn, stock or milk**
- 6 **pork chops**
- ½ **teaspoon salt**

1. In small saucepan, cook onion and celery in shortening, over medium heat until soft, stirring frequently.

2. Combine bread crumbs, KELLOGG'S ALL-BRAN cereal, seasonings, corn and liquid in large mixing bowl. Add cooked onion and celery, mixing lightly. Spread in 10×6×2-inch (1½-quart) glass baking dish or coated with cooking spray. Arrange pork chops over stuffing. Sprinkle with salt. Cover.

3. Bake at 375°F for 30 minutes. Uncover and bake 15 minutes longer or until meat is tender and no longer pink.

Carrot Spice Bread

PREP TIME: 10 minutes ■ **TOTAL TIME: 1 hour 25 minutes**

Makes 1 loaf (about 16 slices)

> 3 cups *Kellogg's Raisin Bran*® Cereal, crushed to 1½ cups
>
> 1 cup orange juice
>
> 4 egg whites
>
> 1 tablespoon vegetable oil
>
> 1 package (18 ounces) moist **carrot cake mix with pudding**
>
> 1 tablespoon powdered sugar

1. In large mixing bowl, combine KELLOGG'S RAISIN BRAN cereal, orange juice, egg whites and oil. Let stand 3 minutes or until cereal has softened. Beat well. Add cake mix, stirring until thoroughly combined. Pour into 9×5×3-inch loaf pan coated with cooking spray.

2. Bake at 350°F for about 1 hour or until wooden pick inserted near center comes out clean. Cool on wire rack 15 minutes. Remove bread from pan; let stand until completely cool. Sprinkle with powdered sugar to serve.

Chili

PREP TIME: 15 minutes ■ **TOTAL TIME: 1 hour 15 minutes**

Makes 6 servings

1	pound lean ground beef
1	large onion, sliced
½	cup chopped green bell peppers
1	cup *Kellogg's® All-Bran® Original* Cereal or 1 cup *Kellogg's® All-Bran® Bran Buds®* Cereal
1	can (16 ounces) red kidney beans, undrained
1	can (16 ounces) whole, peeled tomatoes, undrained
1	can (8 ounces) tomato sauce
½	cup water
1	tablespoon chili powder
⅛	teaspoon garlic powder
1	teaspoon salt
1½	teaspoons sugar
	Bay leaf

In large saucepan, cook ground beef, onion and bell pepper until meat is browned, stirring frequently. Stir in remaining ingredients, cutting tomatoes into pieces with spoon. Cover. Cook over low heat about 1 hour. Stir occasionally. Remove bay leaf before serving.

Sour Cream Bran Coffee Cake

PREP TIME: 15 minutes   ■   **TOTAL TIME: 1 hour 20 minutes**

Makes 8 servings

> 1½ **cups all-purpose flour**
> 1 **teaspoon baking powder**
> ¼ **teaspoon salt**
> 1¾ **cups** *Kellogg's Raisin Bran*® **Cereal**
> 1 **cup sour cream**
> ¾ **cup margarine or butter, softened**
> 1 **cup sugar**
> 1 **teaspoon grated lemon peel**
> 2 **eggs**

1. Stir together flour, baking powder and salt. Set aside. Combine KELLOGG'S RAISIN BRAN cereal and sour cream in small mixing bowl. Let stand about 5 minutes or until cereal is softened.

2. In large mixing bowl, beat margarine, sugar and lemon peel until light and fluffy. Add eggs one at a time, beating well after each addition. Stir in cereal mixture alternately with flour mixture, mixing well. Spread in greased 9-inch tube cake pan.

3. Bake at 350°F about 55 minutes or until wooden pick inserted in center comes out clean. Cool 10 minutes, remove from pan and cool completely. Drizzle with powdered sugar glaze, if desired.

POWDERED SUGAR GLAZE: To make glaze, combine 1 cup powdered sugar with 4 teaspoons warm water.

Banana Cottage Cheese Pancakes

PREP TIME: 15 minutes ■ **TOTAL TIME: 25 minutes**

Makes 4 servings

> 3 **eggs, separated**
> 1 **cup (8 ounces) cottage cheese, drained**
> ¼ **teaspoon salt**
> ⅓ **cup all-purpose flour**
> ½ **cup *Kellogg's® All-Bran® Original Cereal***
> ¼ **cup diced banana**
> **Butter or margarine**
> **Sliced bananas**
> **Hot maple-flavored syrup**

1. In small bowl, beat egg whites until stiff but not too dry. Set aside.

2. In another bowl with the same beaters, beat cottage cheese, salt and egg yolks until nearly smooth. Gradually beat in flour and KELLOGG'S ALL-BRAN cereal. Stir in diced banana. Fold in egg whites.

3. Using about ¼ cup batter for each pancake, cook on greased griddle preheated to 375°F, turning only once. Serve with butter, banana slices and syrup.

Chocolate Chip Craisin® Cookies

PREP TIME: 25 minutes ■ **TOTAL TIME: 1 hour 20 minutes**

Makes 3½ dozen cookies

- 2½ **cups all-purpose flour**
- 1 **teaspoon baking soda**
- ¼ **teaspoon salt**
- ¾ **cup butter or margarine, softened**
- ¾ **cup granulated sugar**
- ¾ **cup firmly packed brown sugar**
- 2 **eggs**
- 1 **teaspoon vanilla**
- ¼ **cup hot water**
- ½ **cup *Kellogg's® All-Bran®* Original Cereal**
- 1 **cup *Ocean Spray® Craisins®* Original Dried Cranberries***
- 1 **package (6 ounces, 1 cup) semi-sweet chocolate morsels**
- ½ **cup chopped walnuts**

*If desired, substitute 1 cup of Ocean Spray® Craisins® Blueberry or Pomegranate Juice Infused dried cranberries for Craisins® Original Dried Cranberries.

1. In medium bowl, stir together flour, baking soda and salt. Set aside.

2. In large mixer bowl, beat butter, granulated sugar and brown sugar on medium speed of electric mixer until light and fluffy. Add eggs and vanilla. Beat well. Mix in hot water. Add flour mixture and KELLOGG'S ALL-BRAN cereal. Beat until combined. Add OCEAN SPRAY CRAISINS DRIED CRANBERRIES, chocolate morsels and walnuts. Mix just until combined.

3. Drop by rounded teaspoonfuls onto cookie sheets coated with cooking spray. Bake at 375°F for 13 to 15 minutes or until golden brown. Remove from baking sheets. Cool completely on wire racks. Store in airtight container.

Almond Butter-Dark Chocolate All-Bran® Muffins

PREP TIME: 20 minutes ■ **TOTAL TIME: 40 minutes**

Makes 18 muffins

1⅓ cups all-purpose flour
½ cup sugar
2 teaspoons baking powder
1 teaspoon baking soda
¼ teaspoon salt
1⅓ cups milk
1 cup *Kellogg's® All-Bran®* Original Cereal
¾ cup regular rolled oats
1 egg, slightly beaten
1 medium banana, mashed (⅓ cup)
⅓ cup crunchy almond butter
½ teaspoon cinnamon
¼ teaspoon nutmeg
1 cup semi-sweet chocolate morsels

1. In medium bowl, stir together flour, sugar, baking powder, baking soda and salt. Set aside.

2. In large bowl, combine milk, KELLOGG'S ALL-BRAN cereal and oats. Let stand about 2 minutes. Add egg, banana, almond butter, cinnamon and nutmeg. Beat well. Add flour mixture and chocolate morsels, stirring until just combined. Portion evenly into eighteen 2½-inch muffin-pan cups coated with cooking spray or lined with foil bake cups.

3. Bake at 375°F for 16 to 18 minutes or until a toothpick inserted in center comes out clean. Let stand in pan for 5 minutes. Transfer to wire rack. Serve warm.